Heartfelt Moments

Sue Donnelly

Heartfelt Moments

Thanks

There are many people I need to thank. Not least those who have embraced the emotion in my poetry, and have laughed and cried with me. I would specially like to thank my family, friends, Wordsmiths and Poetica Christi Press for believing in me long before I believed in myself. Many others have also offered words of advice and experience. Their encouragement has allowed me to discover the poems hidden within.

Heartfelt Moments
ISBN 978 1 74027 865 2
Copyright © text Sue Donnelly 2014
Cover image © Romolo Tavani – Fotolia.com

First published in this form 2014
Reprinted 2016

Ginninderra Press
PO Box 3461 Port Adelaide SA 5015
www.ginninderrapress.com.au

Contents

Injuns	9
She'll be there soon…	10
Hooked	11
Bra Fitting	13
Flashback	15
Turbulations	16
Love	17
A Walk in the Rain	18
Being Mum	20
Whispers of the wind	22
Life at home	23
One step ahead of my shadow	24
Time	25
Corporate Spirituality	28
Between You and Me…	29
Anxiety	30
Depression	31
Lost and Found	32
No one but me	33
Tears	34
Hurt	35
One More Day?	36
Small Dreams	37
Where am I?	38
Pure Love	40
Mum's Suicide	41
Mum	42
Miss you	43
City	44
Richmond	46

Before	47
Heartfelt	48
As One	49
Hhmph!	50
Black Business	51
Masks	52
Peace	53
Baby Lambs	54
blue daffodils	55
Gold Rush	56
Imagine	57
Shakes	58
Me	59
The fridge is sick	60
The Oven	61
Gerald	62
The Spare Pair of Glasses	63
Bullying	64
For You	65
Hide and Seek	66
Freedom	67
Little Ones	68
A different perspective	69
Innocence	70
Listen for…	71
Love is	72
Love Lost	73
Hope	74
Mumbles	75
A worn path	76
Eternal	77
Acknowledgements	78

For Mum

Injuns

Inside
there's still
a little girl

painting David's face
with texta
I told him
you need real warpaint
to be an injun

but his mum didn't like
his warpaint
she screamed
grabbed his ear
scrubbed his face hard
under the tap

she kept screaming
it didn't help
it didn't come off

I said I was sorry
but that didn't help either

David was in Big Trouble
not about the texta
his crime was far worse

he was STUPID
she screamed
to listen to

A GIRL!

She'll be there soon…

I stood

as the back door
sagged
with the heat

ice blocks melting
waiting for her
to come and play

lemonade mess
dripped
into sticky fingers

as flies fought
for ice blocks
slippery sweetness

I tried to shoo them
but I didn't win…

even the sticks
surrendered to the heat

I tried to save them
but she never came…

Hooked

Tassie's craggy rocks
your wave-washed boots
wind-whipped fingers
fishing line

reef-locked line
tangled tight
lures lost   gone
words caught by seagulls

arms bent backwards
my line disappears
green crimplene trousers
securely hooked

rainbow sandals
safe in rock pools
sea limpets win
the tug of war

your size 12 boots
wrinkled with stories
fill blue buckets
full of dreams

morning yawns
marmalade doorstops
vegemite face
buttered crusts in hand

loads of line
from the corner store
exorbitant price
you always say

you stand still
searching
feeling the line
I chatter
'quiet…you'll disturb the fish'

so I talk to them
in excited whispers
it works

I don't wake one fish!

Bra Fitting

my invisible grandma
lives on the edge of the world

but not the paperbarks

paperbark grandmas
live in change rooms

shed cardies like bark
white   wrinkled

hold me in a wobbling mass
of heaving breasts and ample arms

'all women are the same'
Mum said

they're not!

humiliated embarrassed
words stuck like concrete

'you'll soon fill a AA'
whispered Grandma Double E or F

her Riverboat bra
filled with…

bosoms my dad would've called 'em
re-arranged like pockets

for lavender hankies

my invisible grandma
lives in black and white photos

she's not one of the paperbarks

they hover
smiles clinging to walls

where wafts of hairspray and gossip
fall like paperbark

Flashback

I see
a little girl

head between
two fluffy pillows

in a Big Bed
she's me

and I'm
little me

up high
away

there's no ceiling
no sound

just little me
watching little girl

knowing
nothing hurts

any more…

* Forty years after being beaten unconscious at school

Turbulations

Somewhere
In my tumultuous childhood
I found my wings
And took flight…

Love

It was a warm sultry night
when I found you my love
thunder crashed
shards of lightning streaked the sky

as the pavement breathed
steam hovered…
then held the night's secrets
close to the earth

as our fingertips touched
your eyes met mine
though no words were spoken
the joy and heartache of our lives
found rest

we embraced – tenderly, lovingly
lost in each other's arms

we walked till our feet
found no more pavement
and the night called
to the morning sky…

A Walk in the Rain

(Noumea)

we walked
as lovers
alone on a tropical isle
and I held the hibiscus
you picked for me

then it came
each drop a monsoon
heavier and heavier
till well past wet
we sheltered under a ledge
drenched and bedraggled

all the while
I cupped my hands
to protect the hibiscus

water filled my ears
slipped past my lips
till waterlogged
I could taste only monsoonal rain

then came the giggles
like the monsoon they wouldn't stop
and so we walked
you wet and sodden
me bedraggled and giggling

we walked past
the doorman
the concierge
leaving monsoonal puddles
across the vast lobby
and still I giggled

I uncupped my hands
like us
the hibiscus
was waterlogged
we looked into each other's eyes
and embraced

'I Love You'

Being Mum

no time
for me
for sleep
or coffee
or breakfast

just leftovers

but we play
games in the dark
till forever
and you chuckle

and I smile

as I eat mushy food
from tiny fingers
mashed but
given in love

I wear your
macaroni necklace
to the shops
because you ask me

and I gasp
as you race
through the washing
in your plastic car

my hair needs a wash
my trackies smell of
I don't know what

but I know

in your smiles
your grumbles
your hugs of love
are a thousand I love yous

Whispers of the wind

in the wind
are the whispers of the trees

you need only listen

take time today
and listen

with your heart

Life at home

I talked to the TV
today
and yesterday

he understands
shares   debates
my political views

the walls
whimper whisper…
afraid their secrets
will be overheard
they cover them in cobwebs

the taps
have too much to say
they drip constantly…

my husband speaks their language
I fumble to remember
what thingamajig to look for
which whatsit tightens taps
in this organised orchestra of tools

frustrated the taps continue to drip

PLEASE STOP HE'LL BE BACK TOMORROW!

One step ahead of my shadow

when the night was still
and even the moon was asleep
I slipped past my shadow…

shadow snores
louder than possums
blew golden leaves
from their beds
till autumn
settled at my feet

my shadow slept
past breakfast's
marmalade munchings
past lunch
and gossiping coffee mugs

past late afternoon walks
and laughing leaves
steamy soup and stodgy sandwiches

as sunlight snuggled
under every leaf
I finally missed
my snoring friend…

Time

I kissed him goodbye
bleary-eyed my husband
mumbled something into the pillow
his murmurs of love
touched my heart

I tiptoed to
small ones
cocooned in darkness
unseen kisses
fell into unfinished dreams

I wished I could
see their smiles
hear their grumbles
my heart ached
for furry slippers
lost socks
and eyes full of hope

from the soulful silence of my heart
I whispered our children names
and stepped out into the dark
imprisoned by guilt
I fumbled for keys
works relentless demand
for pre-dawn hours
crushed my soul

late that night
shared fears
spilled into waiting arms
too many mornings of tears
and toast left half eaten
upside down smiles
and downcast days
we sat amongst
half empty coffee cups
lives half lived
surrounded by things
exhausted by emptiness

it was summer
our lives were already cold…

I traded pay slips for pillow slips
and found time
for my husband
my children

I could see their smiles
hear their grumbles

as they left me
utterly
alone

I had time
to stare at the dishes
and wait
for them to wash themselves
while the lawnmower and I exercised

I had time
so much time
I felt emptiness echo

I loved my family
but I longed for life…

this morning
while I had coffee
with the vegemite crusts
I decided
the dishes and lawnmower
will have to learn to be alone

tomorrow
my dreams blossom…

Corporate Spirituality

Silk and stilettos
bare their teeth
and swallow
their victims whole

having flossed
applied sincerity
smile to the mirror
hungry for their next victim

Between You and Me...

Gossips are
great encouragers

an elitist hierarchy
they recriminate wrongdoers

leaving you
to right their wrongs

Anxiety

fragile   worn
from the inside out

cracks show as

shaky hands
trembling tears

brokenness

Depression

walking shell
ashen face

movement
but no life

Lost and Found

I live
at the Lost and Found

they're helping me
find myself

and I will
I've been lost before

it's crowded
with disbelief

not everyone
wants to be found

that's why they need
such a large department

No one but me

there's no one here but me
and I don't like myself today

clumsy
bad mood
bad hair day

burnt the toast twice
I'll burn water next

there's no tea
no coffee
and no keys

God help me
find
the keys to peace…

Tears

we say goodbye
perhaps for the last time
and as I walk away
I cry…

as my tears fall
I hear your voice
remember me with smiles and laughter
and I cry even more

warm scones on Friday
wheelchair races Saturday
tired arms, worn shoes
a quick sherry I think…

I can't help but smile

I'll save you a seat in heaven…

I laugh –
one things for sure
you'll talk God's ear off too…

Hurt

I've watched you struggle
for so long

let go

wounds never heal
while the knife
still turns

One More Day?

tortured kisses
agonise

unable to accept
unable to let go

one more breath
one more kiss

anguished eyes
plead with me

there are no words
only tears

I hold him
close my eyes

I can still feel
his last kiss…

Small Dreams

I want to…

walk forward
free from my yesterdays

be in today
without a care for tomorrow

walk under rainbows
that have no end

feel the wind in my hair
as it tousles and tangles

see the sun dancing on water
the moon slumber at sea

skip with autumn leaves
as they swirl in sunbeams

walk without an umbrella
in the monsoonal rain

walk through snowflakes
feel them touch my soul

walk through the fog
with you beside me

hold our children
close to our hearts…

Where am I?

I can't find the moon
or the stars

there is no light
to guide me

only darkness
all around

lost and alone
emptiness

imprisons my heart
shatters my soul

asleep or awake
I do neither well

for there is no living
in the dark

as the sun's breath
touches the earth

hope warms my soul
and I breathe easy

I lie on the grass
for no reason at all

I don't need one
as I listen to

the wind whisper
to my heart

I smile
warmly   deeply

I don't need the moon
or the stars to find my way

I'm there…

Pure Love

Love
in its purest form
loves wholly
deeply
and forever

Cradle
your love
in mercy and
hope not
for a perfect world
but a world
where the imperfect
are loved

Mum's Suicide

memories
wrapped in tears

fall

into a
pool of love

causing

ripples
of hurt and pain

Mum

I've cried out the empty

I try to hold you
but I can't

not even in my dreams

there's no more tears
just pain

I try desperately
to keep you with me

but you've gone

I have to find my way
through the dark…

Miss you

I miss

    squares of cadbury
    to soothe an aching heart

    the way you took time
    to enjoy fine English tea

    plain biscuits no sugar
    it's not good for you – you said

    and you were right

    but when Edith Piaf
    had sung her last note

    there was always more cadbury's
    chocolate's good for you – you said

After your suicide…

    Edith Piaf and I wait
    for her to sing the last note

    there's squares of cadbury on china
    fine tea in your cup

    I can't say goodbye…

City

In the half light
the city still sleeps
the clatter and clang of bins
and barking of dogs
disturb the dishevelled city
not yet ready to wake
he grumbles and groans

wounded by the nights battles
he sees no reason to get up
his streets littered
with lost hope

as the sun pierces the shadows
light unties the strings
that hold them in place
and they slip silently away
while warmth snuggles in the corner

a child's mischievous laugh
wriggles into his heart
and without realising
the city smiles

then
as if from a distance
he watches
the child play
with nothing
and everything

as the child
plays with leaves
dripping with sunshine
the city remembers

his is a world of wonder

Richmond

every now and again
I walk past your life

past the heady aroma
of roses full to overflowing
that entice my senses
and promise abundance

yet not a single petal
ever touches the ground

the cobblestone path
invites me in to uncover its secrets
but the wrought iron gate
remains firmly shut

not a single weed grows
nothing is ever out of place
no toys litter the path
no shoes wait expectantly for a walk

just the yellow pages
plastic wrapped
thrown in by an outsider
waiting like you to flicker to life…

we have never met
you and I
yet I want to run
down the cobblestone path
tear open the plastic wrap
and shout too loudly

Live   Live

Before

Remember this always my darling

before a smile ran across the earth
before laughter chuckled in the valley

I loved you

Heartfelt

the breath of love
soft as gossamer
has entwined
these hearts

bound together
with silken cords
love finds rest
as their souls embrace

the breath of love
love's heartbeat

As One

winter kisses
softened by snowflakes

caressed
by the moon

in an endless
embrace…

Hhmph!

powder pact
nose snorts
disdain drifts
from nasal nostrils

pompous pouting
snobbery sniggers
pretentious pose
Priscilla's pride

Black Business

the stifled
beat of conscience

constrained
constricted

straightjacketed
by profit

Masks

behind the walls
the faces of stone
are the remnants of a people
who have forgotten
how to…

LIVE

Peace

only when
the fight for peace
ends
is peace
truly found

Baby Lambs

buttons of white
nestled in green nurseries
count sheep
in nursery rhyme dreams

blue daffodils

sway against
yellow sky

ochre clouds
burn the horizon

green memories
fade into
red dust

Gold Rush

they lived
with gold in their dreams
dust in their boots
and rum in their bellies

gambling sickness and death
men fought to survive
another day
another hour

for gold

Imagine

red globules
falling into
a planet's silky sky

ebbed tides
pink crystals
winking at the night

as sand stretches
settles
into the night's horizon

Shakes

Our fridge has the shakes. 'Then it must be half off its head like you,' my husband mutters in fun. And he's right. My hands shake from anxiety. I'm an odd bod. Just a bit odder than I used to be.
The fridge doesn't mind about the shakes. It's part of who he is. I don't know if the world gets too much for him or what. But every now and again he shakes and nothing I do changes it. So I hold him and try and remember that he doesn't mind. A freeing of his troubles he calls it.
So I let go and share a coffee with the washing machine. We get together for girl talks now and again. She also gets the shakes – but even more so. She always tears up and then she shakes. She doesn't mean to. She's just insecure. Like me. We hold each other. She shakes in my arms and I shake with her. Everything in my house shakes. So why is it that I find it so hard to accept that I shake too? Why do I feel I have to be the anchor in a world that mostly shakes – if only a little bit?

Me

I sit with my knees bundled up against my chest. My eyes sting as I try and hold back tears.
Slowly I lean my head against the tumble dryer and feel her warmth.

She hums in low slow notes, Safe   Safe   Safe

I'm hiding from myself. Hurt and pain won't stay hidden forever. It always leaks out.

At first only a few tears fall and I can still pretend that I'm strong.
I'm not. I'm broken.

Silent tears become sobs. Sobs become sniffs.
My large fluffy towel is warm and soggy.

The dryer still hums, Safe   Safe   Safe

If I told my husband I need a hug I know he would be there for me. He wouldn't understand this mess of tears. But he would put his arms around me and hold me while I sog up his jumper.

That's what I need to do.

Love myself. Even when I'm weak…

The fridge is sick

The fridge is sick. He used to hum – especially at breakfast. He doesn't say anything any more

He's depressed. The washing machine doesn't shake and whirr when she see's him. And he's sad. He doesn't understand – it's just a game to her.
She wriggles and wiggles and winks at the dryer instead. He has no idea that he too will be dropped, for the ironing board standing tall and proud in the corner.
The fridge is desolate. I hear him groan in his sleep. He thinks I don't know. But every morning there are tiny ice cubes in the fridge and water seeping onto the floor.
My friend is crying…

The Oven

She's hot and passionate and filled with desire. Her lines are sexy and sensual. Her luscious eyelashes flash eyes that burn with fire. I long for just a glance, to be inflamed by her fiery gaze.

I yearn for her dark eyes to look into mine. To be consumed by all that she is…

But she averts her eyes. Ignores my presence.

She longs only for the dishwasher's steamy breath…

Gerald

Gerald collects dog hair and various other bits and pieces from around the house. He has a particular passion for tiny white buttons. He gobbles them up.

Trouble is my vacuum is hyperactive. I can't get him to stop. I literally have to pull the plug. Then he gets the grumps and won't talk to me. He acts like he can't hear a word I say and ignores me completely.

Or he sulks and refuses to start. He says he is too full to move. It doesn't matter how many times I search for dog hairs – he always claims there's one more clogging him up. I know he hasn't broken down and so does he. But I can't prove it and he knows that.

And when I give up he knows he's won.

I hate losing to the vacuum. But it doesn't make sense to keep arguing when I know I've lost. Either way I feel like an idiot!

The Spare Pair of Glasses

I have come to understand you through your glasses.
Sometimes you sit waiting – eyes closed – to move the world and rearrange the pieces. And while you wait your glasses stay high on your head. It is as if there is nothing to see. Well not yet – anyway.
That's when we argue. I try and pull you away from your world of silence to mine of non-stop chatter. You always say it's me who argues. I always say it's you.
I try and talk to you like you're there. But I've lost you to another world. Your world of silent thought.
I know you'll come back. But at the moment I feel alone.
That's why I wear your glasses.
They don't suit me. Your glasses look large oversized on my head. Friends have suggested I get them resized.
But they wouldn't be you then…

Bullying

inside
a little girl

stood silent

too frightened
to speak

too terrified
to cry

their violence
broke me

speak out
please…

For You

listen
little one

know
when your heart

is bleeding
bruised
or broken

I bleed with you

Hide and Seek

a game I play
to hide
pain hurt…

hidden
I shelter
within

till

fragile fearful
I cradle my hurt
in love

Freedom

I found my horizon
my inner self

freed from the limits
of expectation

Little Ones

sticky delights
fingerprint
Christmas windows

fairy floss fingers
adorn
Santa's beard

standing tall
as tables
with Christmas baubles

Innocent hearts
find the wonder of Christmas

A different perspective

trams trundle
in the chaos of Christmas

sparrows
cheekily peck for crumbs

an arthritic hand
touches my shoulder

'scuse me ma'am,
any change at all

gaping grin
excitable eyebrows

$5 fortune
lollipop eyes

Mr 2 teeth's
Christmas dreams

Innocence

trails of tissue
follow
puppies papered
in love

rooms wrapped
in wafts of white
fill puppy paws
with summer snow

Listen for…

God's peace
God's blessing

in the everyday moments
of your life

Love is

kisses and quiet moments
a look across a crowded room
buying flowers in a busy market
feeling lost when they leave too soon
being able to say you're sorry
forgiving the past – and letting go
loving the person inside
finding ways to let them know
seeing sunshine when rain is falling
holding each other in the dark
being there for one another
knowing nothing can keep you apart

Love Lost

You gasped for air – that last long breath
You gasped for air – there was nothing left

I held you in my hand so small
Yet soon there was nothing left at all

A tiny one I once had known
Was now nothing more than skin and bone

Though tiny and small you held my love
Wing heavenwards now my little dove

Hope

the bird bath
has frozen
hope of sun
seems lost

I sleep
in a hammock of hope
waiting for winter
to pass

unexpectedly
sunshine snuggles my shoulders
pulls at my mouth
till a smile is born

mischievous rays
tickle my toes
slide somersault
in the hammock

till tears of joy
flood my face
and laughter
fills my heart

Mumbles

In the unseen hours
I feel his kisses
fall gently on my cheek
and I mumble lovingly
sleepily

but not in English

no whispers
of romantic love
in sensual tones

or lover's smile
or belated kiss

from the long lost
pummels of my pillow
striated with dreams

I mumble
IRUVU

A worn path

leave your troubles
with the dust at the door

and your heart
will find inner peace

Eternal

The winds of love blow
stronger than time

through a summer breeze
or a winter storm

loving endlessly…

Acknowledgements

Some of these poems have been previously published as follows:

'Peace' in *Disarmed*, Jean Sietzema-Dickson and Kathryn Hamann, Poetica Christi Press, 2005

'City' in *Reflecting on Melbourne*, edited by Janette Fernando and Jean Sietzema-Dickson, Poetica Christi Press, 2009

'Time', 'Baby Lambs' in *New Beginnings*, edited by Janette Fernando, Poetica Christi Press, 2010

'Love' in *Everyday Splendour*, edited by Janette Fernando, Poetica Christi Press, 2011

'Lost and Found' in *Horizons*, edited by Janette Fernando, Poetica Christi Press, 2012

'Turbulations', 'Freedom', 'Hope' in *Taking Flight*, edited by Janette Fernando, Poetica Christi Press, 2013

'One More Day' in *Exploring the Depths*, edited by Janette Fernando, Poetica Christi Press, 2013

www.ingramcontent.com/pod-product-compliance
Lightning Source LLC
Chambersburg PA
CBHW062149100526
44589CB00014B/1752